WOULD YOU RATHER?

Christmas edition

© Copyright 2021
FUN FACTORY Publishing

© Copyright 2021
FUN FACTORY Publishing

All rights reserved. No part of this book may be reproduced or used in any manner without the prior written permission of the copyright owner, except for the use of brief quotations in a book review.

HOW TO PLAY

Would You Rather? is a game where you're faced with two scenarios, and you have to choose only one.

One person asks the question and the other person can discuss their answer to the question before choosing between them.

Making a choice can feel impossible!

You'll have lots of fun as you ponder the silly questions and make your challenging choice.

Most important: Remember to have fun and enjoy the game!

WOULD YOU RATHER?

Have Christmas tree tinsel for hair

or

have fingernails that light up like Christmas lights?

Have to wear earplugs

or

wear nose plugs during Christmas dinner?

WOULD YOU RATHER?

All the snowmen you build come alive
or
all the snowballs you throw boomerang back so you can throw them again?

Go for a ride in Santa's sleigh
or
take a ride on the Polar Express?

WOULD YOU RATHER?

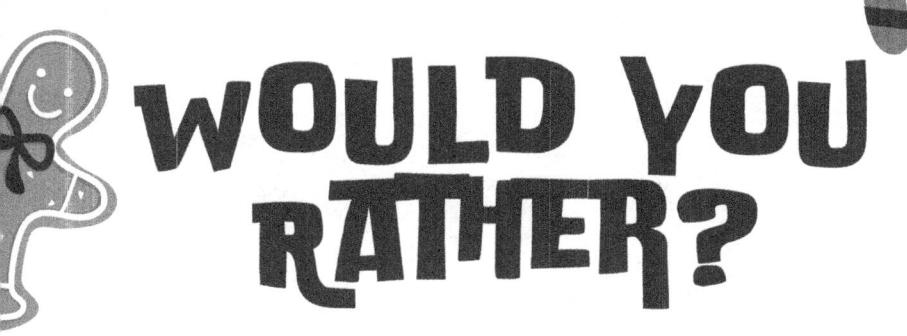

Dress like Buddy from the film Elf

or

have a big white beard like Santa?

eat only this holiday meal over and over
for an entire month

or

eat only fast food?

WOULD YOU RATHER?

Have had to open your presents at 2 am

or

eat Christmas dinner at 2 am?

Have to loudly sing the chorus of "Jingle Bells" every time you walk into a room for a week

or

have to wear a Santa suit to school every day for a week?

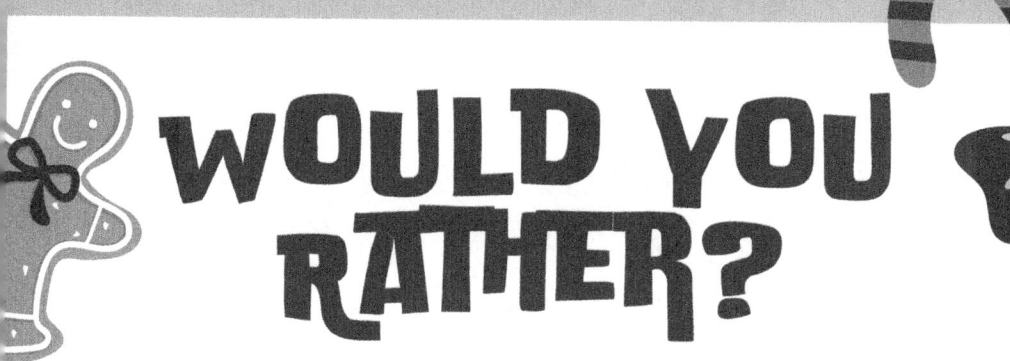

WOULD YOU RATHER?

Have your family over for Christmas

or

go to someone else's house?

Going to school / work wearing an elf hat

or

a red Rudolph nose?

WOULD YOU RATHER?

Fill your entire ceiling with tinsel

or

mistletoe?

Have a holiday party every night of the month

or

no holiday parties to attend?

WOULD YOU RATHER?

Have to call your teacher / boss after dinner to say "Merry Christmas"

or

trip and fall in front of the whole family on your way to the couch?

Wear ugly matching sweaters for the entire month with your family

or

not put up any Christmas decorations at all?

WOULD YOU RATHER?

Santa's red suit to school

or

wear a green elf suit to school?

Smell like Brussels sprouts for a week

or

smell like roast turkey for a week?

WOULD YOU RATHER?

Have snow falling in your bedroom doorway

or

have a large decorated Christmas tree in your bedroom doorway?

Write a five-paragraph essay about the meaning of Christmas

or

solve a page of Christmas-themed math problems?

WOULD YOU RATHER?

Have to wrap 100 presents with the elves

or

load 100 presents into Santa's sleigh?

Eat 75 Christmas cookies

or

drink a gallon of holiday punch?

WOULD YOU RATHER?

Eat a gingerbread house

or

live in a gingerbread house?

Decorate your Christmas tree with all candy canes

or

strings of popcorn?

WOULD YOU RATHER?

Have hair and a beard like Santa

or

be totally bald?

Be best friends with Frosty the Snowman

or

Rudolph the red-nosed reindeer?

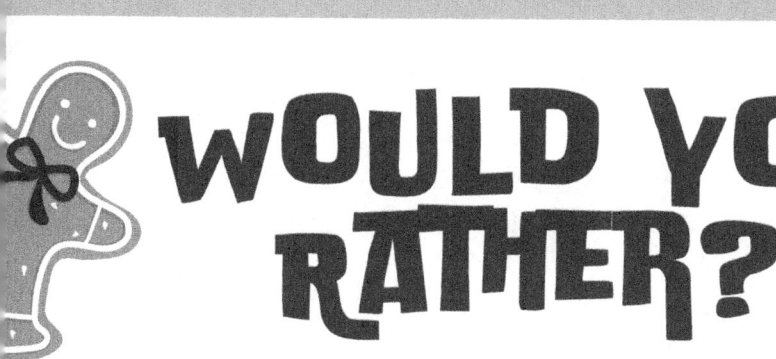

WOULD YOU RATHER?

Have hair and a beard like Santa

or

be totally bald?

Have to run the a 5K race an hour after Christmas dinner

or

clean up the whole kitchen?

WOULD YOU RATHER?

Get many small presents for Christmas

or

get one big present for Christmas?

Have a snowy Christmas

or

a hot Christmas, with no snow at all?

WOULD YOU RATHER?

Get many small presents for Christmas

or

get one big present for Christmas?

Have the outside of your house totally decorated and the inside empty

or

the inside of your house totally decorated and the outside bare?

WOULD YOU RATHER?

Have bright green hair

or

bright red teeth?

Eat Christmas cookies with Santa

or

bake Christmas cookies with Santa?

WOULD YOU RATHER?

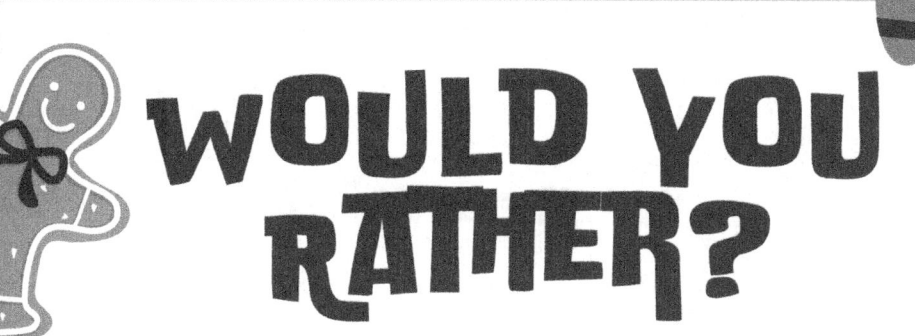

Eat raw onion

or

a clove of garlic?

Have a red nose that lights up

or

have pointy elf ears?

WOULD YOU RATHER?

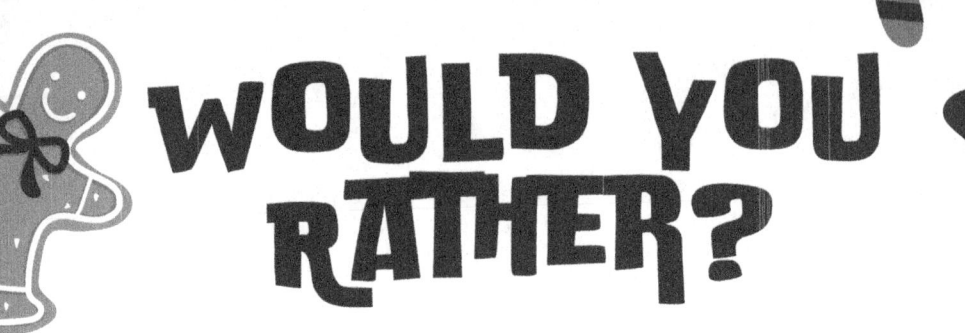

Go flying on the back of a reindeer

or

test some of the toys made by the elves?

Have a job wrapping presents at the mall

or

have a job taking pictures of children sitting on Santa's lap at the mall?

WOULD YOU RATHER?

Sing Jingle Bells once an hour for a week

or

wear bells on the end of your school shoes for a month?

Have to eat candy canes for breakfast, lunch, and dinner for a week after Christmas

or

go to school / work dressed as a candy cane for a week?

WOULD YOU RATHER?

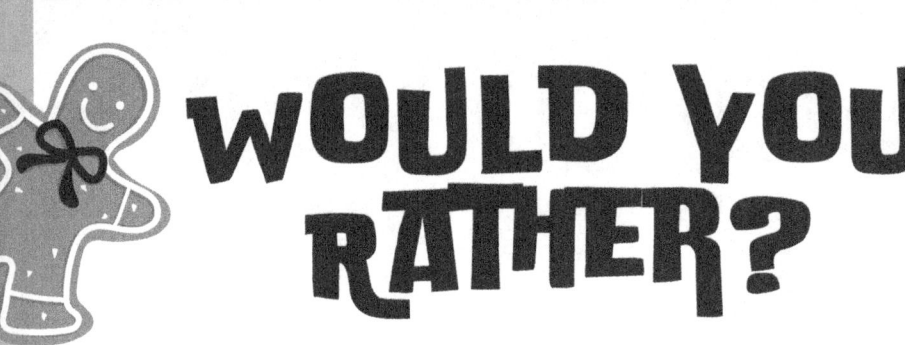

Go forward in time and spend Christmas morning as an adult

or

back in time and spend Christmas morning as a pre-schooler?

Go to school / work dressed as an elf

or

dressed as a reindeer?

WOULD YOU RATHER?

Eat your cereal with eggnog
instead of milk

or

eat a candy cane sandwich?

Be the one to see Santa
come down the chimney

or

be the one to receive
the most presents under the tree?

WOULD YOU RATHER?

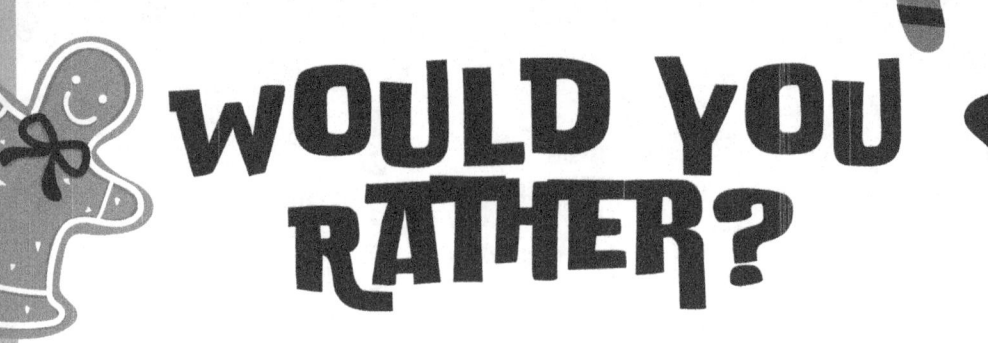

Eat Christmas cookies for 6 months

or

eat candy canes for 6 months?

Be a mouse and receive a BIG piece of cheese for Christmas

or

be a cat and receive a BIG fish for Christmas?

WOULD YOU RATHER?

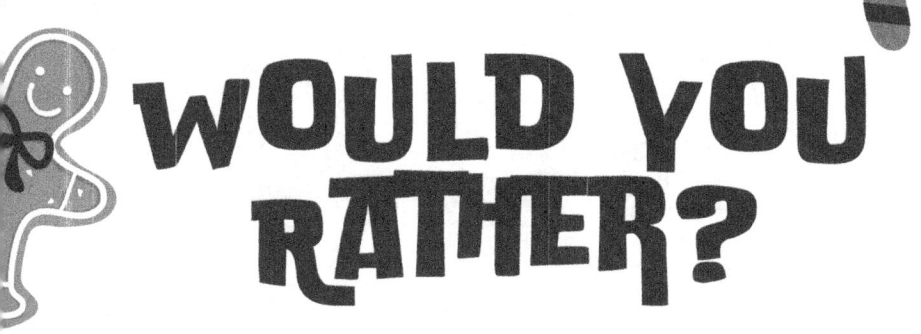

Have a belly that shakes like
a bowl full of jelly

or

eat a bowl full of jelly?

live in a giant gingerbread house

or

ride on the Polar Express?

WOULD YOU RATHER?

Cook a big Christmas dinner

or

do all the washing up?

Wrap a thousand presents

or

bake a thousand cookies?

WOULD YOU RATHER?

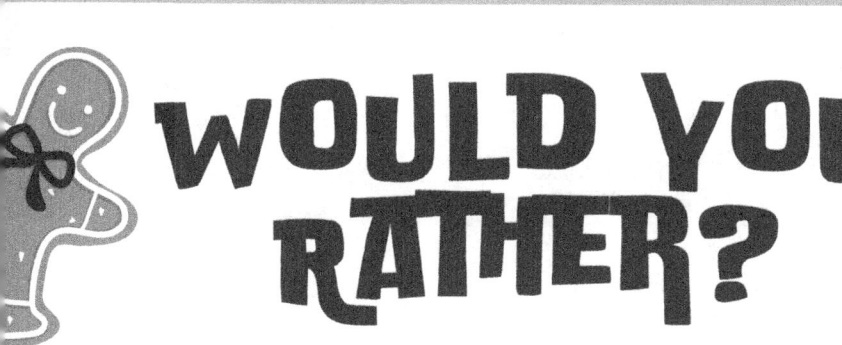

Cook a big Christmas dinner

or

do all the washing up?

Lose your voice for the holidays

or

only be able to speak in Christmas carols?

WOULD YOU RATHER?

Have to eat
only candy canes for a week
or
only Christmas cookies
for a week?

Be stuck in a home that has
no power on Christmas
or
in a house that has no cookies on
Christmas?

WOULD YOU RATHER?

Be able to sit down and eat cookies with Santa

or

spend a whole day at the North Pole with the elves?

Not be allowed to speak on Christmas

or

not be allowed to open your gifts?

WOULD YOU RATHER?

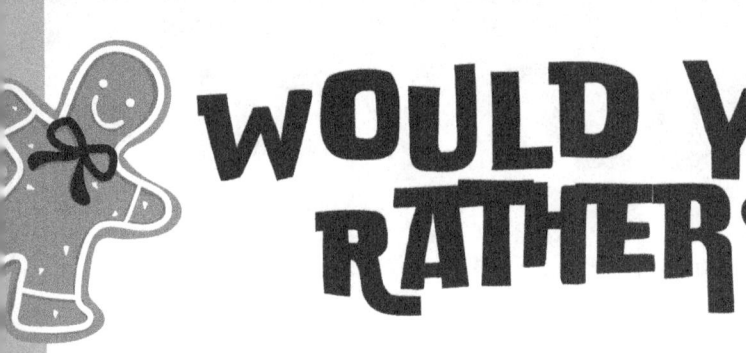

Decorate 100 Christmas trees

or

decorate 100 Christmas cookies?

Have a big belly like Santa Claus

or

have a big glowing red nose like Rudolph?

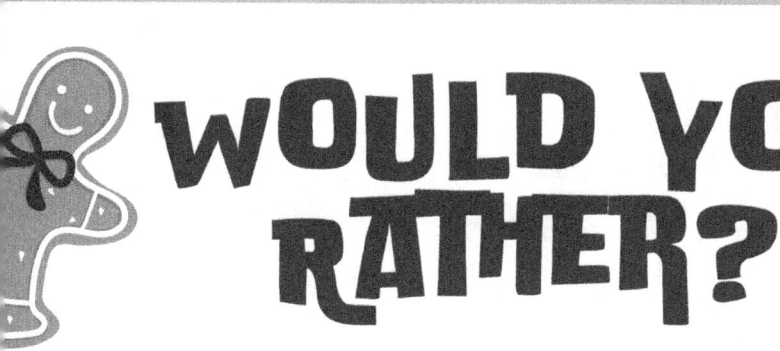

WOULD YOU RATHER?

Decorate 100 Christmas trees

or

decorate 100 Christmas cookies?

Give cash as a gift

or

give a gift that you made for 10 hours?

WOULD YOU RATHER?

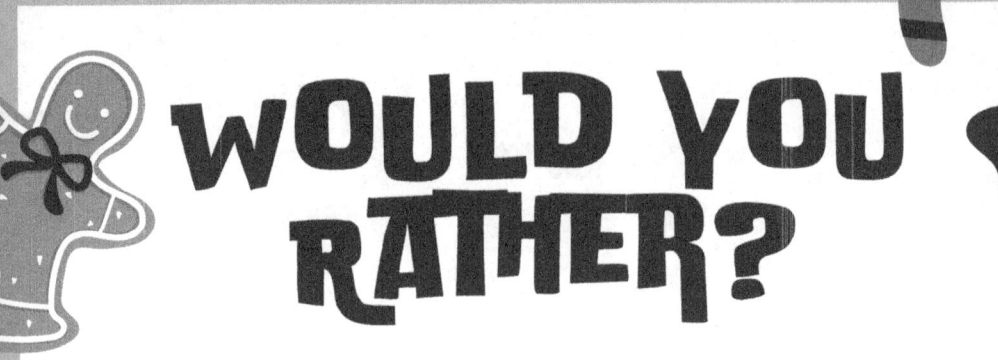

Have snow on Christmas morning

or

a warm 80 degrees Christmas day?

Be covered in Christmas lights

or

in Christmas tinsel?

WOULD YOU RATHER?

Have a constant itch

or

have constant hiccups during Christmas dinner?

Be invited to the White House for Christmas dinner

or

have a celebrity chef come to your house to make your Christmas dinner?

WOULD YOU RATHER?

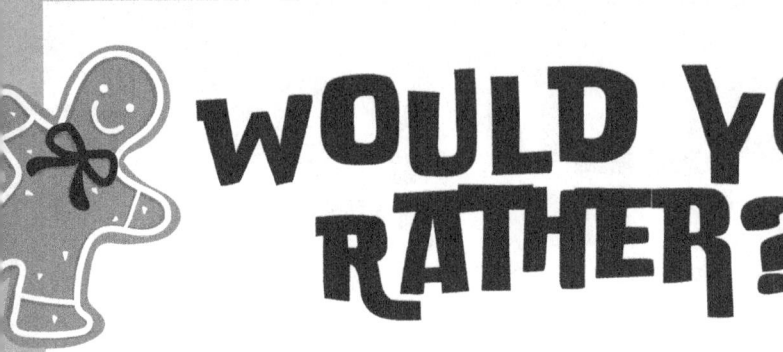

Be able to say "Merry Christmas" in every language in the world

or

know the answer to 500 Trivial Pursuit questions?

Be 30 minutes late to open presents under the tree

or

30 minutes early?

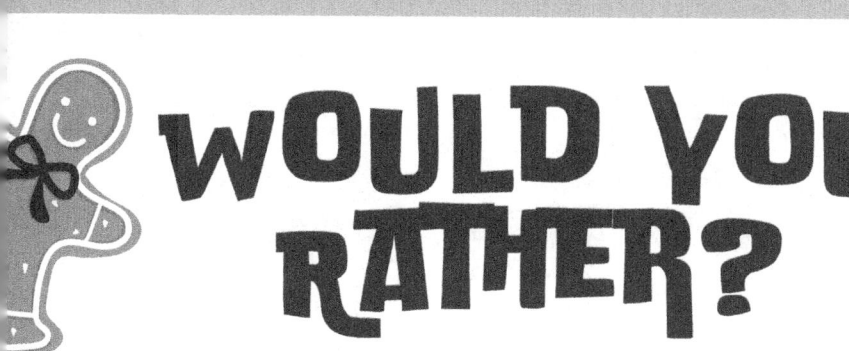

WOULD YOU RATHER?

Have a pet reindeer

or

have a talking snowman?

Receive socks for Christmas

or

receive a dictionary for Christmas?

WOULD YOU RATHER?

Be one of Santa's elves

or

be one of Santa's reindeer?

Wrap 100 presents

or

eat 100 cookies?

WOULD YOU RATHER?

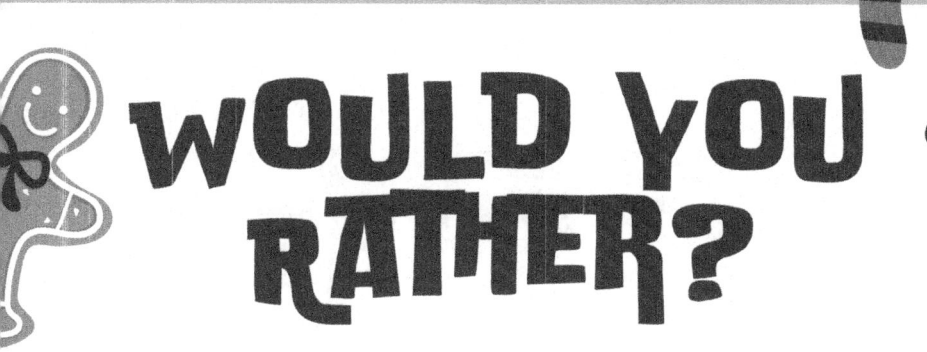

Have one extra gift

or

one extra day off school?

Be gossiped about by your family after
you leave the room on Christmas

or

have them not remember who you are?

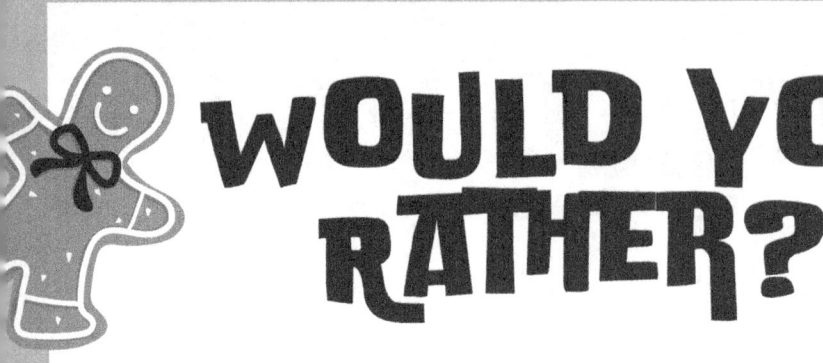

WOULD YOU RATHER?

Open your presents on Christmas Eve

or

on Christmas morning?

Have a red nose like Rudolph

or

have hooves like a reindeer?

WOULD YOU RATHER?

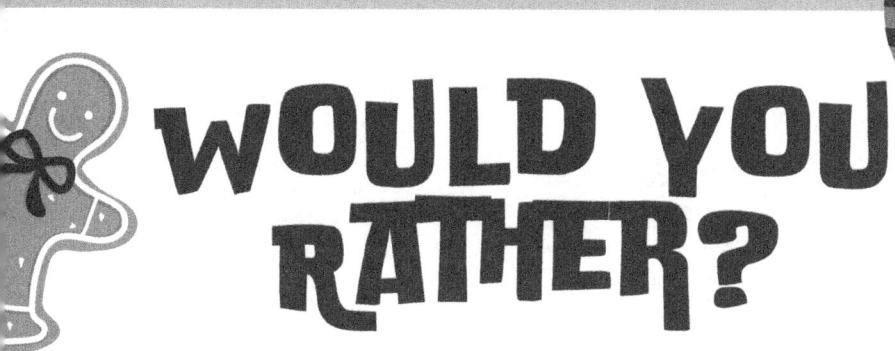

Only be able to sing words
for the whole day
or
just have the ability to say,
"Ho! Ho! Ho!" ?

Go without television, movies, and wifi
during Christmas vacation
or
go without Christmas dinner and cookies?

WOULD YOU RATHER?

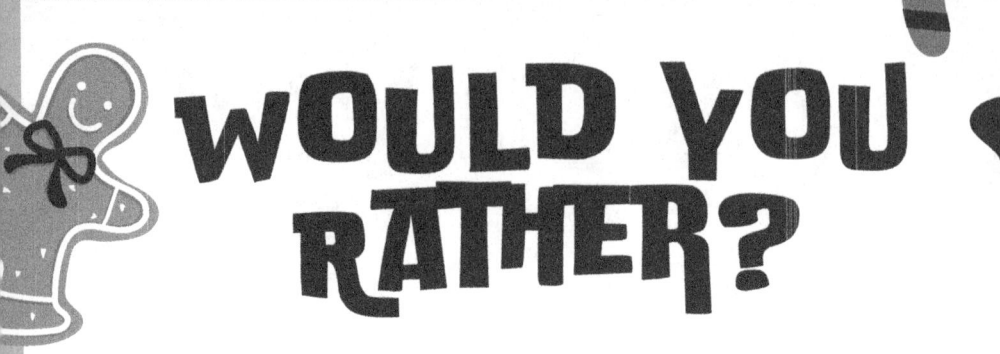

Have turkey for Christmas dinner

or

have a ham for Christmas dinner?

Have chocolate chip cookies

or

sugar cookies?

WOULD YOU RATHER?

Be at home on Christmas and get lots of presents

or

go to Disneyland for Christmas but not get any presents?

Spend a day watching Christmas videos

or

spend a day Christmas shopping at the mall?

WOULD YOU RATHER?

Make snow angels

or

igloo forts?

Be allowed to only eat fruitcake
for two days

or

be allowed to only eat candy or canes for
two days?

WOULD YOU RATHER?

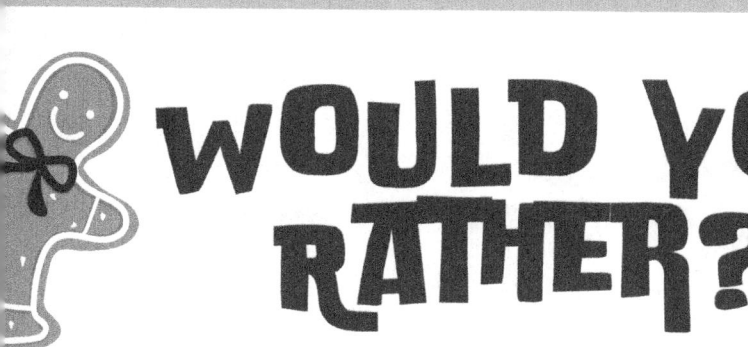

Grow Santa's beard
or
Santa's belly?

Have your favorite athlete join you for
Christmas dinner
or
your favorite TV star?
(And who would it be?)

WOULD YOU RATHER?

Be a dancer in the Nutcracker ballet

or

sing a solo in your school or church's Christmas pageant?

Be a melting snowman

or

a munched on gingerbread person?

WOULD YOU RATHER?

Be a dancer in the Nutcracker ballet

or

sing a solo in your school or church's Christmas pageant?

See The Nutcracker

or

dance in The Nutcracker?

WOULD YOU RATHER?

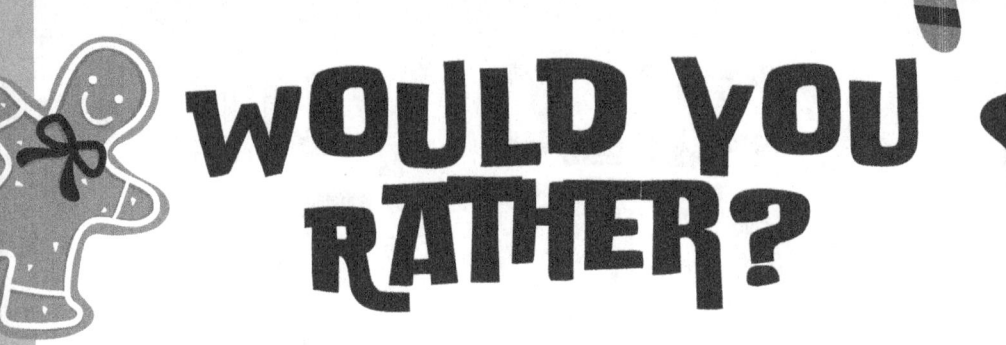

What every single gift you are getting actually is

or

be completely surprised?

Christmas caroling

or

go sledding?

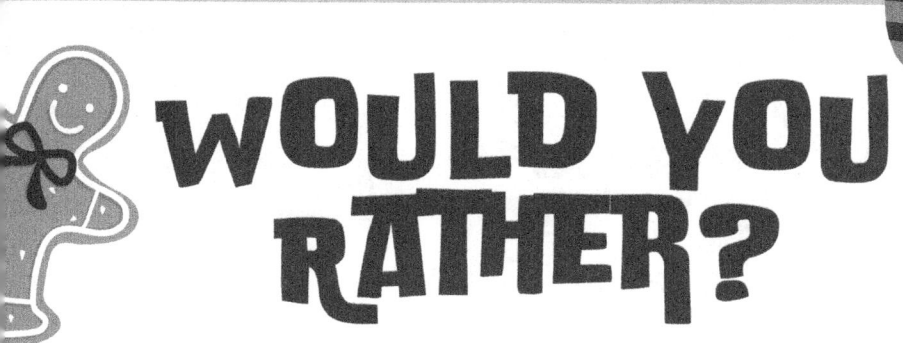

WOULD YOU RATHER?

Be given $100 for Christmas to buy things for yourself

or

be given $1000 before Christmas to use to buy gifts for other people?

Go the entire holiday season without Christmas shows and movies

or

without Christmas music?

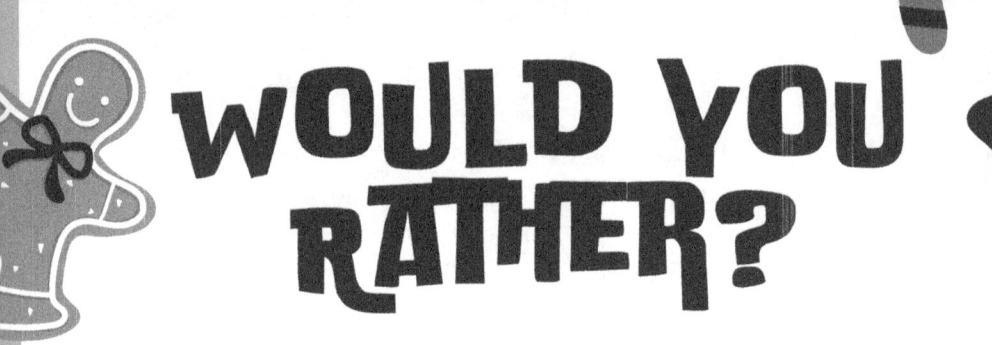

WOULD YOU RATHER?

Spend Christmas in a home without electricity

or

in a home without running water?

Meet Santa Claus

or

visit the North Pole?

WOULD YOU RATHER?

Cunt how many spoonfuls of food are left on the table

or

count how many grains of salt there are left in the salt shaker?

Have a massive snowstorm on Christmas Eve

or

no snow at all?

WOULD YOU RATHER?

Meet The Grinch

or

be The Grinch?

Be Mrs. Claus

or

be the Head Elf in Santa's workshop?

WOULD YOU RATHER?

Have to wear a shirt tomorrow that lists everything you received today

or

lists everything you ate today?

Be an elf working in Santa's shop

or

a reindeer pulling Santa's sleigh?

WOULD YOU RATHER?

Have to say everything you are thinking

or

never be able to speak at all on Christmas Day?

Wear Santa's big boots to gym class

or

wear pointy elf shoes to gym class?

WOULD YOU RATHER?

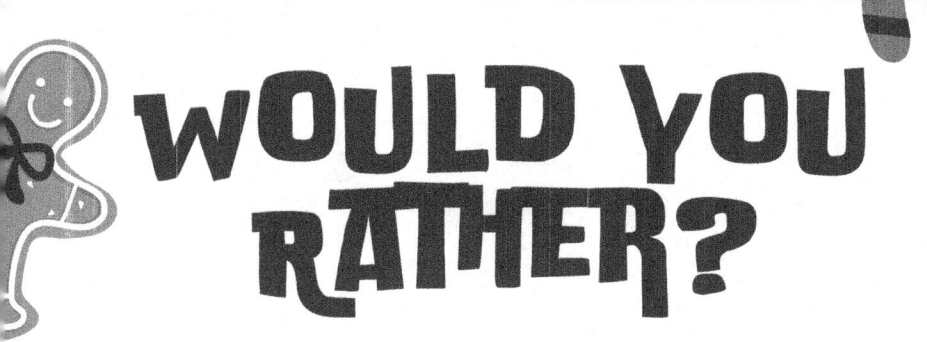

Spend Christmas in the snow

or

spend Christmas at the beach?

Only be able to whisper

or

only be able to shout everything you say on Christmas Day?

WOULD YOU RATHER?

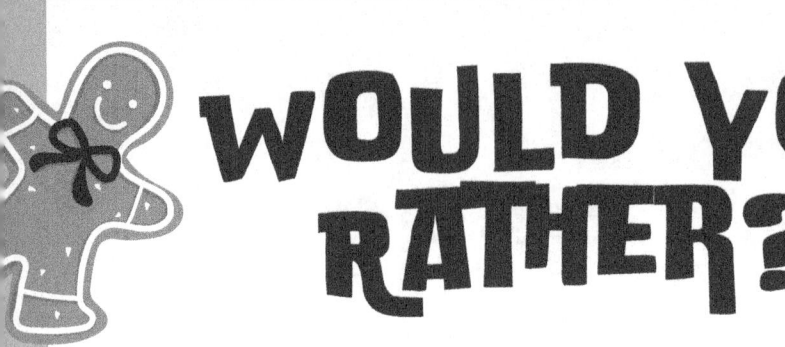

Visit the North Pole

or

visit Bethlehem?

Have the ability to fly like a reindeer

or

the ability to create snowmen that speak?

WOULD YOU RATHER?

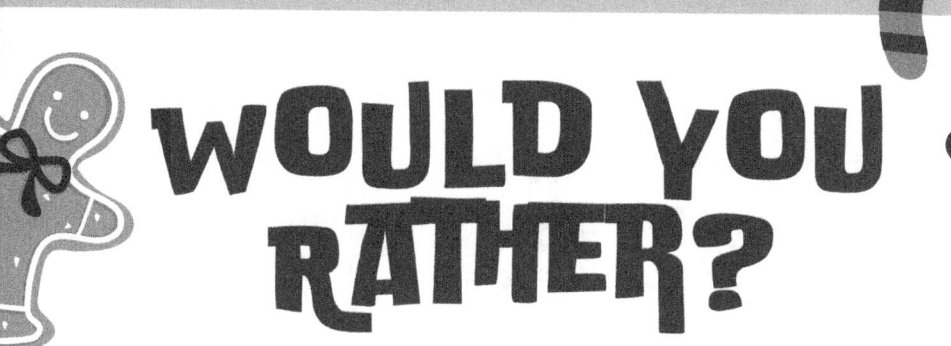

Visit the North Pole

or

visit Bethlehem?

Drink only eggnog all December

or

eat candy canes all December?

WOULD YOU RATHER?

Have the "We Wish You A Merry Christmas" song always stuck in your head

or

dream the very same dream about elves dancing every night?

Sit in a tub of hot chocolate for 6 hours

or

try to stuff 100 marshmallows in your mouth?

WOULD YOU RATHER?

Watch Home Alone on a loop

or

Be home alone for the day so you can do whatever you want?

Swim in a pool of eggnog

or

a pool of warm cocoa?

WOULD YOU RATHER?

Live in a gingerbread house
or
work in Santa's workshop?

Live at the North Pole for a year
or
at the International Space Station for a year?

WOULD YOU RATHER?

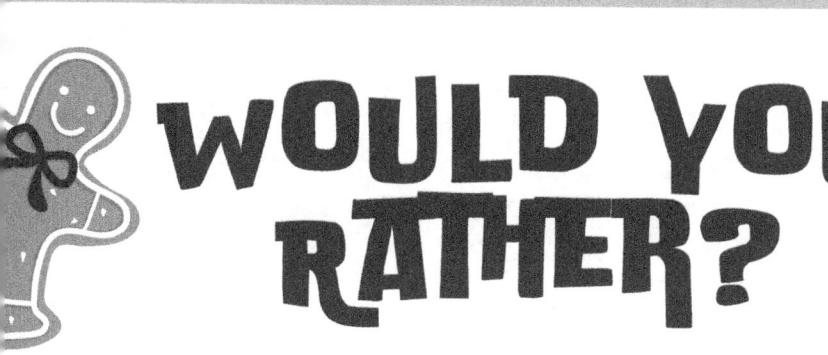

Have reindeer antlers

or

have pointy elf ears?

Be the height of an elf

or

the height of the Abominable Snow Monster?

WOULD YOU RATHER?

Have reindeer antlers

or

have pointy elf ears?

Eat Christmas dinner at home

or

help serve Christmas dinner to those who are less fortunate?

WOULD YOU RATHER?

Spend a day with Mrs. Claus

or

Santa Claus?

Have to read your diary at the Christmas dinner table

or

make a movie of your most embarrassing moment and show it to all of us after dinner?

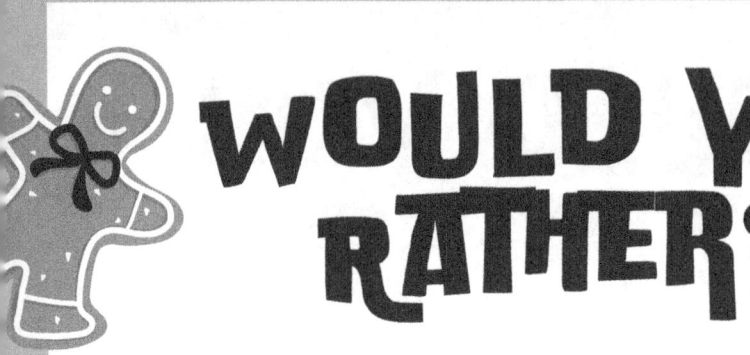

WOULD YOU RATHER?

Spend an entire day just
drinking hot chocolate
or
eating freshly baked cookies?

Wear Santa's red suit
or
one of his elf's outfits outside with
friends?

WOULD YOU RATHER?

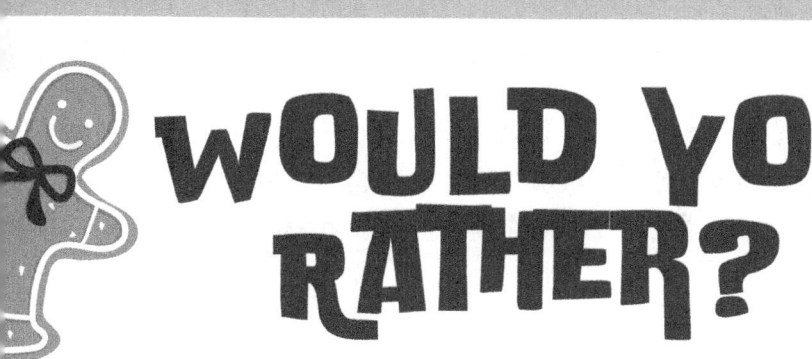

Meet Rudolph

or

meet Jack Frost?

Have to wear your winter coat in the desert

or

your bathing suit at the North Pole?

WOULD YOU RATHER?

Make toys all year long

or

play with toys all year long?

Share your advent calendar chocolate

or

Share your selection box treats?

WOULD YOU RATHER?

Eat ice cream on Christmas

or

eat soup in the summer?

Work in Santa's workshop

or

work in a giant toy store?

WOULD YOU RATHER?

Eat a pound of raw potatoes

or

a pound of raw green beans?

Not celebrate Christmas this year

or

not celebrate your birthday this year?

WOULD YOU RATHER?

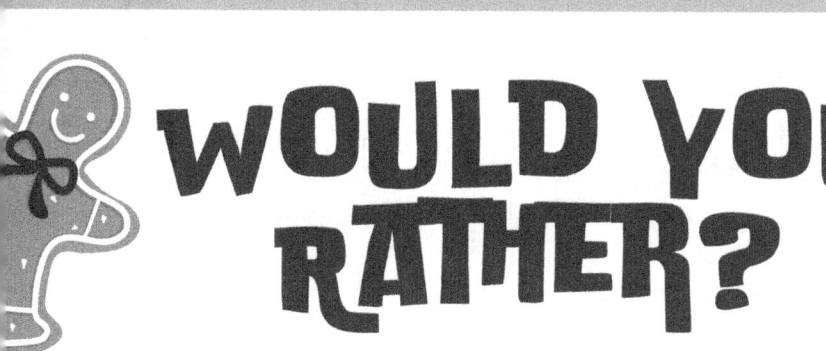

Only be allowed to listen to Christmas carols for a year

or

have to make toys for a year?

Have mistletoe hanging in your bedroom doorway

or

have a large, decorated Christmas tree in your bedroom doorway?

WOULD YOU RATHER?

Have a grumpy little pet gingerbread cookie named Ginger you absolutely can't eat

or

a rather large red and white striped candy cane growing out of your nose

---

Have to give away one of your belongings for every present you receive on Christmas

or

get to buy a new item of your choice for someone else for every present you receive on Christmas?

Made in the USA
Coppell, TX
11 December 2021

68101429R00044